DYING WITH JESUS

D1557075

DYING WITH JESUS
Meditations for Those
Who Are Terminally Ill,
Their Families, and
Their Caregivers

Angela M. Hibbard, I.H.M.

THE LITURGICAL PRESS
Collegeville, Minnesota

www.litpress.org

Cover design by Ann Blattner. Illustrations by Clemens Schmidt.

	2	3	4	5	6	7	8	9

Library of Congress Cataloging-in-Publication Data

Hibbard, Angela M., 1942–
    Dying with Jesus : meditations for those who are terminally ill, their families, and their caregivers / Angela M. Hibbard.
        p. cm.
    ISBN 0-8146-2918-0 (alk. paper)
    1. Terminally ill—Prayer-books and devotions—English. 2. Caregivers—Prayer-books and devotions—English I. Title.

BX2373.S5 H53 2003
242'.4—dc21   2002035253

CONTENTS

PREFACE

These meditations on the final hours of Jesus are intended for use by anyone who is facing death personally or who is accompanying another person on that final journey. My hope is that the dying and those who care for them will find in the passion of Jesus a new depth of union with Christ and a new sense of purpose as they struggle through the difficult task of facing death.

I would like to thank Marie Handley for sharing the invaluable insights she gained in working with terminally ill patients as a chaplain in the cancer unit of Henry Ford Hospital in Detroit, Michigan. Thanks as well to Maria Davis, who encouraged me when my enthusiasm for this project began to lag. Finally, thanks to Mary Ann Dunigan, a cancer patient, who used a first draft of this work and found it helpful on her final journey. May she rest in peace.

INTRODUCTION

—Dying—

Every person living must eventually grapple with the oldest enemy of the human race: death. Whether it comes suddenly or with agonizing slowness, death creates disruption and crisis in the life of everyone connected to it. Medical personnel and psychologists have described the stages through which the dying person moves: denial, anger, bargaining, depression, and finally acceptance. There are also descriptions of the tasks the dying must accomplish: experiencing love of self and others, completion of relationships, acceptance of the finality of one's life, and the achievement of a new sense of self. No one moves smoothly through the stages nor do people necessarily experience them in the "proper" order. Likewise, many people never accomplish the final tasks of life. Even so, anyone connected to the dying process will witness to the fact that it is a labor and has the dignity which accompanies any great task.

—Dying with Jesus—

Christianity's answer to the mystery of death lies not in science or philosophy or a plan of action but in a relationship. In the person of Jesus we see God's intense desire for union with us. In coming to know him personally and in discovering his presence with us in all things, we can find comfort both in life and in death. The Scriptures tell us that he is like us in all things except sin; but he is also—in the words of the Nicene Creed—"God of God, Light of Light, True God of True God." This Mighty One in whom we believe has shared our process of growth and change, our experiences of family and friends, our struggles to accomplish a life-task, and in the end our physical pain and death. We believe that he will also share resurrection with us on the other side of death.

For Christians the story of Jesus' life serves as a lens through which we can look differently at the events of our own lives. For those who are coming near to death, meditation on the passion and death of Jesus can be particularly enlightening and comforting. Because he was human, Jesus passed through all the phases any person experiences in the dying process. Long before his passion he began to grapple with the reality of his coming death and to prepare his disciples to face and accept it. His struggle with fear, his pleading for deliverance are dramatically clear in the garden of Gethsemane just before his arrest. At the end his final acceptance of death and his willingness to forgive those who killed him is also clear.

—How to Use This Booklet—

Dying with Jesus is meant for people who are dying and for their caregivers, whether family members or pastoral care professionals. Each page contains a Scripture passage with a brief commentary, a meditation intended to capture the thoughts and feelings of the dying person, and a response from Jesus. The booklet can be used as a single extended meditation or it can be read a page at a time in any sequence that is helpful. Page headings indicate the theme found in the meditation and can guide the user to the appropriate page for a given moment.

The meditations are rooted in the experience of dying people, and they may help to identify and give words to many painful thoughts and feelings. By reading a given meditation together chaplains, family members, or the dying person may be able to initiate a difficult but necessary conversation. It is hoped that this set of Scripture texts, dialogues, and prayers will reveal some of Jesus' human struggle and will make it accessible to all who are facing the same frightening reality. All who use it are especially encouraged to share the feelings and memories it calls forth. This gift of shared experience will enlighten those who accompany the dying and will create a bridge between the gospel story and those of us who hear it today.

DIAGNOSIS
fear, anger, confusion

—Jesus Is Condemned to Death—

We adore you, O Christ, and we praise you
Because by your holy cross you have redeemed the world.

—Scripture Passage—

Pilate said to [the crowd], "Then what shall I do with Jesus who is called 'Messiah'?" All of them said, "Let him be crucified!" Then he asked, "Why? What evil has he done?" But they shouted all the more, "Let him be crucified!"

So when Pilate saw that he could do nothing, but rather that a riot was beginning, he took some water and washed his hands before the crowd, saying, "I am innocent of this man's blood . . . ." After flogging Jesus, he handed him over to be crucified (Matt 27:22-24, 26).

Notes on the Text: Pilate, as the lawful Roman authority in Jerusalem, had final responsibility for Jesus' death sentence. Matthew portrays him in a dilemma. Pilate was convinced that Jesus was innocent, but he was also responsible for civil order. Condemning Jesus to death seemed to be the only way to prevent a riot among the people. Washing his hands was a ritual gesture showing his refusal to take moral responsibility for an innocent man's death.

—Meditation—

I remember the day I received my death sentence, Jesus. It was terrifying. It still is terrifying, but I feel more and more weary of the effort to get well.

I want to live too, though. How can I leave everything, everyone I care about? It was confusing then, and it is still confusing.

Is God punishing me? I think that sometimes, and perhaps I deserve it, since I've been so angry about being sick. But have I really done anything bad enough to deserve a death sentence?

Help me to accept this dying I'm doing. Help me find some peace.

—Jesus Speaks—

My Beloved, I am with you now. I have always been with you—when you were well and now that you are sick. I too remember the day I knew I was going to die, but it was long before the high priest and Pilate said the words. And I too was angry, angry that the religious leaders would not listen to me—would not listen to the truth. I know I was doing my Father's will, but my obedience couldn't save me from death. Dying is part of life.

THE ROAD
fear, ambivalence, disorientation

—Jesus Takes Up His Cross—

We adore you, O Christ, and we praise you
Because by your holy cross you have redeemed the world.

—Scripture Passage—

They went to a place called Gethsemane; and he said to his disciples, "Sit here while I pray." He took with him Peter and James and John, and began to be distressed and agitated. And he said to them, "I am deeply grieved, even to death; remain here, and keep awake." And going a little farther, he threw himself on the ground and prayed that, if it were possible, the hour might pass from him. He said, "Abba, Father, for you all things are possible; remove this cup from me; yet, not what I want, but what you want" (Mark 14:32-36).

Notes on the Text: During his final days in Judea, Jesus would stay overnight in Bethany, a few miles from Jerusalem. He would come to the temple area during the day to teach the crowds who were beginning to gather for the annual Passover feast. In the evening before he returned to Bethany he would often take time to pray in the Garden of Olives. On this occasion, his prayer shows that he was deeply afraid to die, and he wanted and needed the support of his disciples as he tried to face that fear.

—Meditation—

Lord, I know that right now my cross is this dying I'm doing—and I'm not sure I carry it very well.

I don't know who I am anymore. I don't have a normal life. Every anchor I had is gone—my work, my ability to keep up my home, all the things I loved to do—and I don't know how to get my feeling of wholeness back again. I get so impatient with myself—and no one around me can really help with the things that make me afraid. I'm afraid to live like this. I'm afraid to die in pain.

Jesus, help me to carry this cross of dying.

—Jesus Speaks—

Beloved, I am with you in your fear. You see that I was afraid too. I wanted to believe that my Father could change the hearts of my enemies, that he could make them see that what I offered the people was good. But they didn't want to see my goodness. God could not violate their freedom, so I had to go to the cross.

WEAKNESS

dependency, anger, depression

—Jesus Falls the First Time—

We adore you, O Christ, and we praise you
Because by your holy cross you have redeemed the world.

—Scripture Passage—

Out of the depths I cry to you, O LORD.
   Lord hear my voice!
Let your ears be attentive
   to the voice of my supplications!
If you, O LORD, should mark iniquities,
   Lord, who could stand?
But there is forgiveness with you,
   so that you may be revered.
I wait for the LORD, my soul waits,
   and in his word I hope;
My soul waits for the Lord
   more than those who watch for the morning,
   more than those who watch for the morning
    (Ps 130:1-6).

Notes on the Text: Psalm 130 is the sixth of the seven penitential psalms, and it expresses well the desperation and sadness felt by someone weighed down by illness and sin. It also expresses the reliance on God which will more and more become the abiding need of those who face death.

—Meditation—

I feel so helpless sometimes, and it angers and embarrasses me. I see others who have to be taken care of like babies, and I dread that kind of dependency. More and more I find that I can't do some things for myself, that I have to let someone else clean up the messes I make.

You said we needed to become like children, but I never thought it could be so literally true. Help me, Jesus, to accept this falling into childhood.

—Jesus Speaks—

Beloved, take my hand. I will wait with you when you call for help.

Can you remember the children's faces you have seen? Look at their trust, their happiness at being held and cared for. Know that I freely became a servant for you and that I am still ready to serve you in this dependency. Trust and happiness and joy are waiting for you here in my hands.

FAMILY
wanting to communicate,
fearing to communicate

—Jesus Meets His Mother—

We adore you, O Christ, and we praise you
Because by your holy cross you have redeemed the world.

—Scripture Passage—

Simeon blessed [the child's mother and father] and said to his mother Mary, "This child is destined for the falling and rising of many in Israel, and to be a sign that will be opposed so that the inner thoughts of many will be revealed—and a sword will pierce your own soul too" (Luke 2:34-35).

Notes on the Text: Simeon was an old man who had been present in the temple when Mary and Joseph came to offer the sacrifice of purification on the fortieth day after Jesus' birth. Scripture tells us that Mary pondered these words in her heart. Surely she remembered them when she met her son on the way to his execution.

—Meditation—

Jesus, what about my family? What will happen to them when I'm gone? I know it's hard for them to see me getting weaker. It's hard for me too when we're together. When I'm too tired to talk and everyone is silent, I wonder what they're thinking. Then sometimes when they do talk I want them to be quiet because they're talking about things that don't involve me any more. What's worse is when they pretend that everything is normal.

Nothing is normal anymore—and so many important things need to be said before I die. I know this family so well, and I see my own sins in them. How can I warn them? How do I say I love you? Thank you? How do I ask forgiveness? And how can I ever say goodbye?

—Jesus Speaks—

Beloved, ask my Mother to stand next to you as she stood with me in my suffering. She taught me to respect every person, so much of my ministry came from that gift of honoring people whom no one else honored. She taught me to ponder the hard questions of life in my heart, so much of what I said to my disciples was the fruit of that pondering. She taught me that God came first before everything, so I lived and died for my Father.

She will help you speak, and she will help you be silent. And she will help you find peace about your family.

CAREGIVERS I
respect, disrespect, self-respect

We adore you, O Christ, and we praise you
Because by your holy cross you have redeemed the world.

—Scripture Passage—

After mocking him, they stripped him of the purple cloak and put his own clothes on him. Then they led him out to crucify him. They compelled a passer-by, who was coming in from the country, to carry his cross; it was Simon of Cyrene (Mark 15:20-22).

Notes on the Text: Before he condemned Jesus to death, Pilate had him scourged. He was weak from loss of blood and was simply unable to survive carrying his cross to the place of execution without help. Simon was not one of Jesus' followers, but the soldiers forced this strange "discipleship" on him without his wanting or expecting it.

—Meditation—

Jesus, were you glad about Simon's help or did you resent the fact that you needed it? I know I feel both ways sometimes. I've had to be lifted and carried, and I'm sure I will be lifted and carried some more before this is over.

Some helpers are so respectful and gentle. They treat me like a person. And some of them make me feel as though my needs are an intrusion and I'm no more important than a sack of potatoes.

Help me to let them help me. Help me to be grateful.

—Jesus Speaks—

Beloved, I am carrying you. Remember that all the Simons who lift you will need to be carried themselves one day. Even the strong are in my hand, whether they know it now or not. Pray for them, since you understand what it means to be carried. And thank them graciously so that they can begin to understand that the weak who are carried have as much dignity as the strong who carry them.

CAREGIVERS II
gratitude for comforters

We adore you, O Christ, and we praise you
Because by your holy cross you have redeemed the world.

—Scripture Passage—

"Lord, when was it that we saw you hungry and gave you food, or thirsty and gave you something to drink? And when was it that we saw you a stranger and welcomed you, or naked and gave you clothing? And when was it that we saw you sick or in prison and visited you?" And the king will answer them, "Truly I tell you, just as you did it to one of the least of these who are members of my family, you did it to me" (Matt 25:37-40).

Notes on the Text: Jesus' parable about the judgment of the nations asserts that a service done for someone in need is a service done to him.

—Meditation—

O Jesus, I'm very grateful sometimes when someone notices what I need without my asking. It is so comforting to have my face wiped or lotion rubbed on my hands—but it's only people who are really paying attention, and who aren't afraid of me because I'm dying, who notice when those things need doing.

I'm glad to think that someone saw what you needed and did it for you.

—Jesus Speaks—

Beloved, my true image is found in those who are hungry and thirsty and naked and sick—so it is found in you. But those who serve you reveal me too, since I am the true image of God, who is love. Your needs move them to compassion, so the true nature of God is made visible when you give and receive service.

Be sure to thank those who serve you. Your gratitude carries a gift of healing in it.

ISOLATION
fear of abandonment

—Jesus Falls the Second Time—

We adore you, O Christ, and we praise you
Because by your holy cross you have redeemed the world.

—Scripture Passage—

My God, my God, why have you forsaken me?
   Why are you so far from helping me, from the words
      of my groaning?
O my God, I cry by day, but you do not answer;
   and by night, but find no rest.
O Lord, do not be far away!
   O my help, come quickly to my aid! (Ps 22:1-2, 19).

Notes on the Text: The gospel writers used Psalm 22 throughout the passion narrative to help them express Jesus' final sufferings. The psalmist's intense isolation and feelings of helplessness are dramatically presented in this portion of the text.

—Meditation—

Jesus, I think about you falling even though you were surrounded by all those people, and I realize how easy it is to be abandoned.

I just can't manage much for myself now, and I'm out of the stream of purposeful activity. Sometimes even when there are people near me I feel as though I'm invisible to them. They are kind enough, and I want to be grateful and hospitable, but it takes so much energy. When I don't say anything the distance grows.

Those around me will go on, but I won't. In a way, I'm abandoning them too. The people I love will also be left alone without me.

Lord, don't you abandon me. Don't you abandon them.

—Jesus Speaks—

Beloved, I am with you day and night. Your weakness is no obstacle to me, and the narrowness of your life now does not shut me out. When you have no energy to be grateful or hospitable, I see your desire and it is enough.

I know you feel as though your illness separates you from others, but if you remember me in my suffering, it will bring you closer to me.

THE BLIND ONES

impatience, grief, weariness

—Jesus Meets the Women of Jerusalem—

We adore you, O Christ, and we praise you
Because by your holy cross you have redeemed the world.

—Scripture Passage—

A great number of the people followed [Jesus], and among them were women who were beating their breasts and wailing for him. But Jesus turned to them and said, "Daughters of Jerusalem, do not weep for me, but weep for yourselves and for your children. For the days are surely coming when they will say, 'Blessed are the barren, and the wombs that never bore, and the breasts that never nursed.' Then they will begin to say to the mountains, 'Fall on us'; and to the hills, 'Cover us.' For if they do this when the wood is green, what will happen when it is dry?" (Luke 23:27-31).

Notes on the Text: The empty mourning displays of the women reveal a kind of sentimentality which weeps for Jesus' pain but is unable to face the true causes of his suffering. The Jewish leaders who are putting him to death have taught the people to serve a false god of judgment. In his quoting of the eighth-century prophet Hosea (Hos 10:8), Jesus again warns Israel to recognize and return to the compassionate God whom he has revealed.

—Meditation—

I know that I'm dying, but some people around me seem to refuse to accept that. They talk about hoping for miracles—but all I want now is peace. There are others who don't seem to know I'm human and have feelings. They talk about me as though I weren't there or as though I were a child who couldn't understand what people are saying. And then there are those—people I thought cared about me—who haven't come or called or sent a card. Nothing.

Help me to forgive them all.

—Jesus Speaks—

Beloved, my true disciples share my cross, and you are surely bearing the same burden of misunderstanding which I suffered. My closest followers all ran from me. The leaders of my own people arranged my death. The wailing women of Jerusalem stood there weeping for my pain and for the shameful death to come. But my loneliness and my feelings of failure were more painful even than that. My heart ached for them and for their children.

PAIN
letting go, depression

—Jesus Falls a Third Time—

We adore you, O Christ, and we praise you
Because by your holy cross you have redeemed the world.

—Scripture Passage—

Now my soul is poured out within me;
    days of affliction have taken hold of me.
The night racks my bones,
    and the pain that gnaws me takes no rest.
With violence he seizes my garment;
    he grasps me by the collar of my tunic.
He has cast me into the mire,
    and I have become like dust and ashes.
I know that you will bring me to death,
    and to the house appointed for all living
        (Job 30:16-19, 23).

Notes on the Text: The author of the book of Job explores the mystery of "undeserved" suffering in an attempt to make some sense of it. In the end, Job's pain remains a mystery which cannot be explained by human reason.

—Meditation—

The medical people ask me how much pain I'm in, and they prescribe doses of medication to keep me comfortable. What do I tell them about the pain of losing my life, my work, my home, my family—and the pain of wondering if my life has been good enough. What can I take for that?

I'm not very brave, and I'm not sure I can get through all this very successfully. Lord, do you have a balm for my spirit?

—Jesus Speaks—

Beloved, remember my agony in the garden before any of the physical pain began. My suffering there came from my sense of failure and hopelessness. I had no more time to proclaim the reign of God—and so little had changed in the three years since my baptism in the Jordan.

Enter my pain and let it strengthen and comfort you.

STRIPPED
shame, depression

—Jesus Is Stripped of His Garments—

We adore you, O Christ, and we praise you
Because by your holy cross you have redeemed the world.

—Scripture Passage—

They brought Jesus to the place called Golgotha (which means the place of the skull). And they offered him wine mixed with myrrh; but he did not take it. And they crucified him, and divided his clothes among them, casting lots to decide what each should take (Mark 15:22-24).

Notes on the Text: The combination of wine and myrrh was administered as a narcotic to help the condemned person endure his suffering. Executioners were allowed to take the personal belongings of those they put to death. Crucifixion was not only a painful but a humiliating death, since the person was stripped naked and left exposed until they died, which sometimes took several days.

—Meditation—

I'm beginning to understand what it feels like to be stripped naked. Not only is my body exposed like a child's sometimes, but all kinds of my personal business is now being taken care of by other people. Some days I feel like I'm losing my mentality too. I say and do things that really aren't me. My memory, my awareness, my energy, my dignity are all slipping away like sand.

Can you hide me from prying eyes?

—Jesus Speaks—

Beloved, remember that nothing about you has ever been hidden from me—your sins, your private thoughts, the things you preferred to do in the darkness are all clear before me. Do not be afraid of this stripping. It is bringing you down to your essential core. Little by little it is making you aware that for your very existence you depend on me.

INEVITABILITY
regret, depression

—Jesus Is Nailed to the Cross—

We adore you, O Christ, and we praise you
Because by your holy cross you have redeemed the world.

—Scripture Passage—

I am poured out like water,
    and all my bones are out of joint;
my heart is like wax;
    it is melted within my breast;
my mouth is dried up like a potsherd,
    and my tongue sticks to my jaws;
    you lay me in the dust of death (Ps 22:14-15).

Notes on the Text: These words of Psalm 22 evoke both the physical suffering and the absolute powerlessness Jesus experienced as he hung on the cross. Crucifixion was a Roman form of execution reserved for slaves, rebels, and the worst criminals. No one survived being nailed to the cross.

—Meditation—

Lord, this is so final. It is worse than the death sentence. You are unable to turn back now that you are nailed to the cross—and I am unable to turn back from this work of dying. I wish I could. There are things I would do differently, say differently. Some of my sins still haunt me because they have left permanent wounds.

Help me to face the inevitability of death. Help me to trust in your mercy.

—Jesus Speaks—

Beloved, I still carry the marks of those nails. They will never fade, but they will forever unite me with all who are wounded. It is true that some sins leave permanent marks in you and in those you have sinned against. But my mercy is greater than your sin.

LAST BREATH
fear, the beginning of acceptance

—Jesus Dies on the Cross—

We adore you, O Christ, and we praise you
Because by your holy cross you have redeemed the world.

—Scripture Passage—

It was now about noon, and darkness came over the whole land until three in the afternoon, while the sun's light failed; and the curtain of the temple was torn in two. Then Jesus, crying with a loud voice, said, "Father, into your hands I commend my spirit." Having said this, he breathed his last (Luke 23:44-46).

Notes on the Text: Luke puts the words of Psalm 31 into Jesus' mouth, a psalm which closely resembles Psalm 22 in that it expresses great suffering—"My strength fails because of my misery, / and my bones waste away" (Ps 31:10)—and great confidence in God's help.

—Meditation—

O Jesus, it makes me so afraid to think of breathing my last breath. What will become of me? Will anyone be there? Will anyone be watching? Will anyone welcome me?

I can't know the answers now, I realize, but I ask you to be with me—help me to commend my last breath into your hands.

—Jesus Speaks—

Beloved, I have received each breath you have taken from first to last. You are safe in me. Trust those who love you to ease your body's struggle—for the body never wants to die—and trust me to ease your spirit as you pass completely into my hands.

EMPTINESS

surrender, acceptance, safety

—The Body of Jesus Is Taken Down from the Cross—

We adore you, O Christ, and we praise you
Because by your holy cross you have redeemed the world.

—Scripture Passage—

O Lord, all my longing is known to you;
    my sighing is not hidden from you,
My heart throbs, my strength fails me;
    as for the light of my eyes—it also has gone from me.
But I am like the deaf, I do not hear;
    like the mute, who cannot speak.
Truly, I am like one who does not hear,
    and in whose mouth is no retort (Ps 38:9-10, 13-14).

Notes on the Text: Psalm 38, one of the group of seven penitential psalms, expresses well the gulf that separates the dead from the living. Communication is no longer possible, neither speaking nor hearing.

The living do not know the peace of those beyond death; they only know their own sorrow and longing.

—Meditation—

Jesus, what will become of everything after I am gone? All the things that surround me in this illness will be useless then. My chair will be empty. My bed will be empty. My clothes, my shoes, my favorite things. . . . And what will become of those who have lost me? I worry that their hearts will be empty too.

Lord, fill them with your comfort. Fill them with gratitude that I am safe with you.

—Jesus Speaks—

Beloved, the space you took in their lives and hearts will never be completely filled, and they will always remember and miss you. Ask my Mother to pray for them. Even as she held my dead body in her arms, she felt the power of the coming resurrection sustaining her. She can help them in their grief.

MYSTERY

acceptance of death

—Jesus Is Laid in the Tomb—

We adore you, O Christ, and we praise you
Because by your holy cross you have redeemed the world.

—Scripture Passage—

When it was evening, there came a rich man from Arimathea, named Joseph, who was also a disciple of Jesus. He went to Pilate and asked for the body of Jesus; then Pilate ordered it to be given to him. So Joseph took the body and wrapped it in a clean linen cloth and laid it in his own new tomb, which he had hewn in the rock. He then rolled a great stone to the door of the tomb and went away. Mary Magdalene and the other Mary were there, sitting opposite the tomb (Matt 27:57-61).

Notes on the Text: Joseph of Arimathea is mentioned in all four Gospels as the one who provided for Jesus' burial. The women who watched at the tomb could not embalm the body then, since the Sabbath was about to begin. They planned to return when it was over. Jesus can no longer feel their touch or experience the passage of time. He has moved into the painless eternal now of death.

—Meditation—

So quickly the space you took in this world is being erased. You are gone from the hill of Calvary and hidden away in the earth.

I hate to think about it, but I know that when the time comes I will be placed in a body bag, in a hearse, in a coffin—and gradually the marks of my existence will fade. I can't imagine what existence without time and space and bodiliness will be like. But then I don't suppose an acorn can imagine life as an oak tree, either.

Lord, help me to be silent in the face of this mystery.

—Jesus Speaks—

Beloved, trust in me. Your presence in this world has left its mark, although your work and your life seem small and insignificant. Your place beyond this world is prepared, and I will welcome you home when it is time.

HOPE
trusting acceptance

—The Resurrection—

We adore you, O Christ, and we praise you
Because by your holy cross you have redeemed the world.

—Scripture Passage—

On the first day of the week, at early dawn, [the women] came to the tomb, taking the spices that they had prepared. They found the stone rolled away from the tomb, but when they went in, they did not find the body. While they were perplexed about this, suddenly two men in dazzling clothes stood beside them. The women were terrified and bowed their faces to the ground, but the men said to them, "Why do you look for the living among the dead? He is not here, but has risen" (Luke 24:1-5).

Notes on the Text: The angels, the two witnesses required by Jewish law, announce the resurrection to the women who come to embalm

Jesus' body. Jesus' physical body has not decayed but has passed totally into the realm of spirit. Now he is no longer bound to one place and time but is free to be with all those who believe in him.

—Meditation—

Lord, all my life I have said, "I believe in the resurrection of the dead," but what can it possibly mean? How can I be me without a body? Without this face, this hair, these hands, these eyes. When will it happen and how will it feel?

I know my questions have no answers now. Again, give me a silent heart, a trusting heart.

—Jesus Speaks—

Beloved, this resurrection is already present in you. You entered into it on the day of your baptism and it will be fully revealed in your death. Even those who sorrow at your passing will in time understand it, because your relationship with them will not be ended, only changed.

Trust in me.

TRADITIONAL PRAYERS

—Our Father—

Our Father in heaven,
hallowed be your name.
Your kingdom come.
Your will be done
on earth as it is in heaven.
Give us this day our daily bread,
And forgive us our trespasses,
as we forgive those who have trespassed against us.
And lead us not into temptation,
but deliver us from evil. Amen.

—Matt 6:9-13

—Hail Mary—

Hail Mary, full of grace, the Lord is with you.
Blessed are you among women,
And blessed is the fruit of your womb, Jesus.

Holy Mary, Mother of God,
Pray for us sinners now and at the hour of our death. Amen.

—Luke 1:28, 42

—Glory Be—

Glory be to the Father and to the Son and to the Holy Spirit,
as it was in the beginning, is now, and will be forever. Amen.

—Apostles' Creed—

I believe in God, the Father almighty, creator of heaven and earth,
and in Jesus Christ, his only Son, our Lord,
who was conceived by the Holy Spirit
born of the Virgin Mary,
suffered under Pontius Pilate,
was crucified, died and was buried.
He descended into hell,
the third day he rose again from the dead,
he ascended into heaven,
and sits at the right hand of God, the Father almighty.
From thence he shall come to judge the living and the dead.
I believe in the Holy Spirit, the holy Catholic church,
the communion of saints, the forgiveness of sins,
the resurrection of the body,
and life everlasting. Amen.

—Memorare—

Remember, O most gracious Virgin Mary, that never was it
known that anyone who fled to thy protection, implored thy
help, or sought thy intercession was left unaided. Turn then,
most gracious advocate, thine eyes of mercy towards us and after
this, our exile, show unto us the blessed fruit of thy womb, Jesus.
O clement, O loving, O sweet Virgin Mary.

Pray for us, O Holy Mother of God,
That we may be made worthy of the promises of Christ.

—Prayer of Abandonment—

Father, I abandon myself into your hands;
do with me what you will.
Whatever you may do I thank you; I am ready for all, I accept all.
Let only your will be done in me, and in all your creatures.
I wish no more than this, O Lord.
Into your hands I commend my soul;
I offer it to you with all the love of my heart, for I love you, Lord,
and so need to give myself, to surrender myself into your hands
without reserve, and with boundless confidence,
for you are my Father.

—Charles de Foucauld

—Favorite Psalms—

The LORD is my shepherd, I shall not want.
    He makes me lie down in green pastures;
he leads me beside still waters;
    he restores my soul.
He leads me in right paths
    for his name's sake.

Even though I walk through the darkest valley,
    I fear no evil,
for you are with me;
    your rod and your staff—
    they comfort me.

You prepare a table before me
    in the presence of my enemies;
you anoint my head with oil;
    my cup overflows.

Surely goodness and mercy shall follow me
   all the days of my life,
and I shall dwell in the house of the LORD
   my whole life long.

—Psalm 23

As a deer longs for flowing streams,
   so my soul longs for you, O God.
My soul thirsts for God,
   for the living God.
When shall I come and behold
   the face of God?
My tears have been my food
   day and night,
while people say to me continually,
   "Where is your God?"

These things I remember,
   as I pour out my soul:
how I went with the throng,
   and led them in procession to the house of God,
with glad shouts and songs of thanksgiving,
   a multitude keeping festival.
Why are you cast down, O my soul,
   and why are you disquieted within me?
Hope in God; for I shall again praise him,
   my help and my God.

My soul is cast down within me;
   therefore I remember you
from the land of Jordan and of Hermon,
   from Mount Mizar.
Deep calls to deep
   at the thunder of your cataracts;
all your waves and your billows
   have gone over me.

By day the LORD commands his steadfast love,
   and at night his song is with me,
   a prayer to the God of my life.

I say to God, my rock,
   "Why have you forgotten me?
Why must I walk about mournfully
   because the enemy oppresses me?"
As with a deadly wound in my body,
   my adversaries taunt me,
while they say to me continually,
   "Where is your God?"

Why are you cast down, O my soul,
   and why are you disquieted within me?
Hope in God, for I shall again praise him,
   my help and my God.

—Psalm 42